Help Your Child 1

CW01391443

Mister Wolf

ALLAN AHLBERG and ANDRÉ AMSTUTZ

GRANADA
London Toronto Sydney New York

Help Your Child To Read

Parents <u>can</u> help their children to start reading. It is not difficult, <u>nor</u> is it necessary to be a trained teacher. In many ways home is a better place to start than school. In school your child will share the teacher's time with 25 or 30 others. At home he can have your undivided attention.

The series HELP YOUR CHILD TO READ is a set of books for parents to <u>share</u> with their children. The books contain stories, rhymes and games. Also, on page 3 of each book, there are practical suggestions for parents: ways in which they can help their children to start reading.

Labels

Writing labels for objects in and around the house is a good way of helping children to read. If you say the word 'door' to your child, he'll understand you. If you write it for him on a postcard and attach it to the door, he'll understand that too. After a while he'll probably remember the word – he'll 'read' it; also 'table', 'chair', 'telephone' or any other label you and he decide to make.

Later you could play at swopping the labels around. One of you makes the swop; the other has to spot what's happened, and correct it. A final point: when making labels, let your child watch you as you write. This will help him too.

What's the time, Mr Wolf?
the children said.
Eight o'clock, said Mr Wolf.

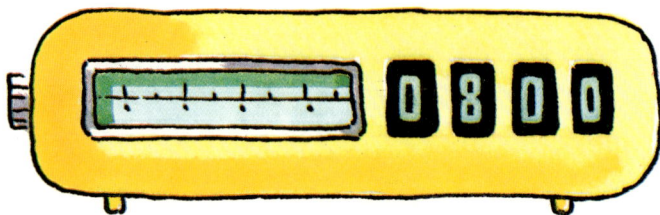

Time for breakfast
bib and cup.
Time for me
to eat you up!

But it wasn't.

What's the time, Mr Wolf?
the children said.
Twelve o'clock, said Mr Wolf.

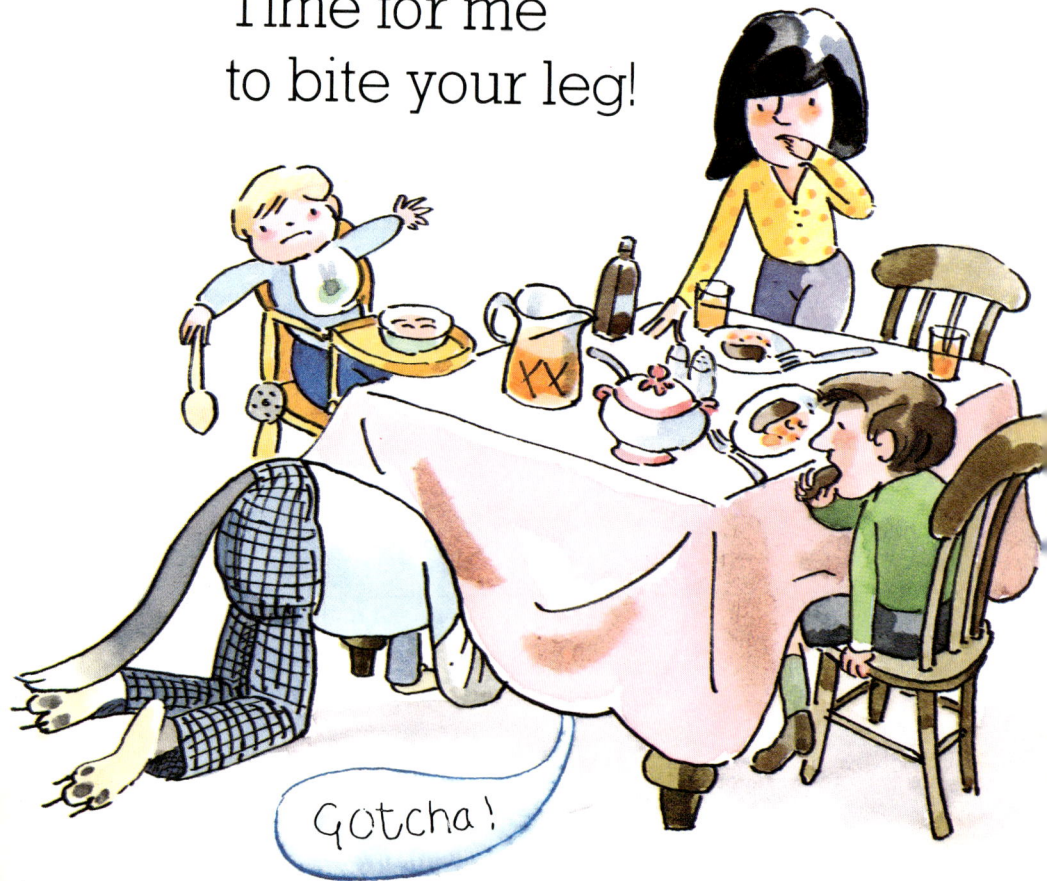

Time for sausage
beans and egg.
Time for me
to bite your leg!

Gotcha!

But it wasn't.

Where am I?

What's the time, Mr Wolf?
the children said.
Four o'clock, said Mr Wolf.

Time for tea
and buttered scones.
Time for me
to grind your bones!

But it wasn't.

What's the time, Mr Wolf?
the children said.
Half past six, said Mr Wolf.

Time for supper,
bath-time too.
Time for me
to swallow you!

But it wasn't.

Oh Grandma, what big lumps you've got!

What's the time, Mr Wolf?
the children said.
Seven o'clock, said Mr Wolf.

Time for story,
time for bed.
Time I had
some crisps instead!

And it was.

Eight o'clock

Twelve o'clock

Four o'clock

Seven o'clock

Published by Granada Publishing Limited in 1983
ISBN 0 246 11860 1 (cased)
      0 583 30551 2 (limp)
Copyright © Allan Ahlberg and André Amstutz
Granada Publishing Limited
Frogmore, St Albans, Herts AL2 2NF
and
36 Golden Square, London W1R 4AH
515 Madison Avenue, New York, NY 10022, USA
117 York Street, Sydney, NSW 2000, Australia
60 International Blvd, Rexdale, Ontario, R9W 6J2, Canada
61 Beach Road, Auckland, New Zealand

Printed and bound in Spain by
Graficas Reunidas S.A., Madrid

Granada ®
Granada Publishing ®